Railway Memories

YORK

Ernest Sanderson

BELLCODE BOOKS
10 RIDGE BANK TODMORDEN
LANCASHIRE OL14 7BA

Before resignalling in 1951 a magnificent collection of North Eastern Railway slotted signals controlled from seven mechanical boxes stood guard over the York approaches. This double arm example and one of the area's smaller manual boxes were at South Points, Dringhouses.

Copyright © 1988 Ernest Sanderson and Bellcode Books.
ISBN 1 871233 003
Edited by Stephen Chapman.
Printed by Netherwood Dalton & Co., Huddersfield.
Published by Bellcode Books, 10 Ridge Bank, Todmorden, Lancashire OL14 7BA.

FRONT COVER: The south end of York station immediately after the formation of British Railways in 1948 with class V2 2-6-2 No. 978, still in LNER livery, setting off for Doncaster. On the right is Queen Street loco shed hosting another V2 and D49/2 4-4-0 No. E2770 "The Puckeridge."

BACK COVER (bottom): A pair of ex-Great Northern Railway large boilered Atlantics, No. 4438 leading, storm past Dringhouses with a King's Cross express in the 1930's. (C. Ord)

BACK COVER (top): Waiting to leave platform 3 with a 1950's express to Manchester via Normanton is ex-LMS Black Five 4-6-0 No. 44791. The locomotive is something of a stranger to York, being based at Glasgow Corkerhill depot.

THE AUTHOR

When Ernest Sanderson first drew breath in 1912, his lungs would have filled straight away with the atmosphere of steam.

The son of a crossing keeper, he was born into York's best known railway community, the Leeman Road area that was exclusively home to many North Eastern Railway employees and their families.

Just a few yards away were the East Coast main line, York's vast North locomotive sheds, bustling marshalling yards and carriage sidings. Even the midwife who brought him into this world of railways was married to an engine driver whose great grandfather was Stephenson's fireman on the Rocket.

Before he could walk, the infant Ernest had already ridden on the footplate and as a growing child frequently visited his father's gatebox at Copmanthorpe Moor level crossing.

More than 75 years later he still lives near the site of the crossing where he grew up, within view of the main lines south from York.

When leaving school there was no doubt that he would work on the railway and in 1927 he joined the London and North Eastern Railway as a track relayer. He was still in the same line of work, but promoted to chargeman, when he retired in 1977.

Ernest's work renewing the permanent way took him all over the York District Engineer's area, which reached from Shaftholme Junction and Moorthorpe in the south, to Thirsk in the north, to what is now the North Yorkshire Moors Railway in the east, and to Garforth, Wetherby and Starbeck in the west.

It was after starting work that he also began photographing the railway around him, at first using his father's camera, a Kodak Autographic Junior. In 1937 he had saved up enough of his £2 weekly wage to buy an Agfa Karat 35mm costing nine guineas. Later he bought a Voigtlander 3½" × 3½", which he still has along with a Rolleiflex twin lens reflex and three Pentax 35mm cameras.

Ernest would take his camera to work and while his mates were having their snap he would be snapping the rich variety of locomotives which in those days seemed to parade by almost continuously. They ranged from ancient North Eastern 4-4-0's to the mighty Garratts of the London Midland and Scottish Railway.

For over half a century Ernest Sanderson has been able, often from a position of considerable advantage, to record on film – and glass – a railway scene that has since changed beyond all recognition.

Because of the vantage point from which many of his pictures were taken, he has also recorded how tracklaying, now a highly mechanised operation, used to be accomplished by sheer hard labour.

Today Ernest Sanderson, Freeman of York, Friend of the National Railway Museum and active member of the Permanent Way Institution, continues to photograph the ever-changing railway scene around York.

We are privileged to bring you his collection which shows this world-famous railway junction in its heyday.

As well as providing sheer nostalgic enjoyment we hope it will form a lasting tribute to the work of Ernest Sanderson, railwayman and photographer.

A RAILWAY METROPOLIS

York's position almost exactly half-way between the English and Scottish capitals, and at a natural meeting point for routes from the Midlands, South West and Lancashire, was to ensure the city a leading role in the growth of railways.

The great Victorian entrepreneur George Hudson – the "Railway King" – dreamed of a main line to London Euston by way of his North Midland Railway, and the Midland Counties and London and Birmingham railways. However, the coming of the Great Northern Railway from London in 1850 posed a serious challenge to this prospect. It also helped make York a more important railway centre than even Hudson could have imagined.

The city's first railway was the York and North Midland which opened in stages during 1839 and 1840. It ran from a terminus just outside the city walls to Normanton where it met the North Midland which ran from Leeds to Derby.

Next on the scene was the Great North of England Railway whose line to Darlington opened in 1841. Three years later intervention by Hudson saw a line completed northwards to Gateshead, connecting York with Tyneside. Also in 1841 a permanent joint station was opened inside the city wall by the YNM and GNE companies.

More railways, mostly promoted by Hudson, followed in quick succession. Lines opened to Scarborough in 1845, to Market Weighton in 1847 and to Knaresborough in 1848. The Market Weighton line was extended to Beverley in 1865, making a through route to Hull, while the line to Selby avoiding the need for Great Northern trains to use part of the Lancashire and Yorkshire Railway to reach York, was opened in 1871. Completing the scene in 1869 was a spur from Church Fenton, on the York and North Midland line, to the Leeds-Selby line at Micklefield giving a more direct route to Leeds, a short branch to a cattle station at Foss Islands, in the east of York, in 1879, and in 1913 the independent Derwent Valley Light Railway from Layerthorpe to Cliff Common, near Selby.

In 1877 the North Eastern Railway, into which the early companies had merged in 1854, opened a massive new through station topped by an awe-inspiring roof of five magnificent arches. The biggest of these stood 48ft high and had a span of 81ft.

Throughout much of the steam age expresses stopped there to change engines and, in the days before restaurant cars, so that passengers could grab a hasty meal at the refreshment rooms.

The York and North Midland Railway founded a locomotive works at Queen Street, just outside the city walls, which repaired locomotives until the early part of this century. A wagon works was set up east of the original GNE line in the 1860's and a carriage works, which grew to massive proportions, on the opposite side along the Poppleton Road in the 1880's.

The YNMR and GNER both had engine sheds at what is now York South and along with three roundhouses built in the 1850's and 60's they formed the North Eastern locomotive depot there. After the NER's 'new' sheds were opened at York North in 1877, the Great Northern moved into the old GNE shed at York South and the Midland Railway into the newest of the three roundhouses. One of the 1850's roundhouses was destroyed by fire in the 1920's but the other two and the GNE shed survived until the end of 1963. Following closure of the loco works in the early 1900's, the Lancashire and Yorkshire Railway turned the boiler shop into a shed for its locomotives which worked across the Pennines from Blackpool and Liverpool.

For over 70 years since the present station was opened York's railways held a steady course with few major alterations other than the sort of expansion which reflected a growing railway industry. Then in 1951 the most modern and biggest route relay interlocking signalling system in the world was completed. Some of the world's most impressive mechanical signal boxes gave way to just one control centre situated in the station, while the towering gantries of NER

OPPOSITE: A bird's eye view of York station area taken about 1937. Bottom left are Leeman Road coal depots which closed in the 1960's when domestic coal was concentrated at Foss Islands freight depot. Immediately above them is Leeman Road tunnel beneath the station's northern approach. Working left to right we can see Branches Yard where local freight trains were handled until the 1960's. The new island platform 15/16 is under construction between Branches Yard and the station. To the bottom right of the station are the former Queen Street locomotive works erecting shops, and inside the city walls the 1841 station. The scene is dominated by the Royal Station Hotel, above the station, the 1906 NER headquarters, overlooking the old station, and the Minster. *(Authors collection)*

wooden slotted signals that had stood guard over the station approaches for many decades were swept aside in favour of neat and efficient colour lights.

The 1960's, with the end of steam traction and the Beeching purges in which lines and stations seemed to close almost daily, brought the next great chapter in York's railway story.

Luckily, York got off lightly from the ravages of Beeching. The only one of its immediate railways to close was the Beverley line in November, 1965; but the run-down of local freight traffic saw a reduction in facilities for such operations, closure of the branches yard on the west side of the station being one example. However, a new hump marshalling yard opened at Dringhouses in 1961 for dealing with modern fully braked express freight trains was getting steadily busier.

This era of change continued into the 1970's as many redundant goods and steam facilities were removed, culminating in the conversion of the North roundhouse into the National Railway Museum which then took over the freight depot on the opposite side of Leeman Road. In 1983 it bought from British Rail the last remnant of York North engine sheds – the well-equipped repair depot which lost all its main line locomotive maintenance work at the end of 1981.

The same year the 1871 Selby line was replaced by a new high speed route which now carries East Coast expresses around the Selby coalfield and the mining subsidence which would otherwise have slowed them to a crawl.

Now York is entering a new bitter-sweet phase in its railway history as perhaps the biggest changes seen this century shape it for the challenge of the future.

The long-awaited electrification of the East Coast main line is well under way and the overhead wires now reach the city limits. As this book is published, work will be starting on an £18 million project that will see York's complicated railway layout drastically slimmed down and the 1951 signalling replaced by a highly sophisticated solid state interlocking system.

The modernised Clifton carriage depot has already closed, made redundant by the replacement of trans-Pennine locomotive-hauled trains with multiple units maintained at Leeds, while Dringhouses marshalling yard too has closed, its work switched to Doncaster.

Likely by the end of 1988 is the sale into private ownership of the huge carriage works and complete closure of the Foss Island branch.

By the time this latest round of changes is complete the scenes in the following pages will be just fading memories to older generations and virtually unknown to anyone under 30.

In 1966 the last two Peppercorn class A1 4-6-2's in BR service were stationed at York. One of them, No. 60124 "Kenilworth", leaves York with the daily empty coaching stock train to Finsbury Park in the 1950's, when it was a Gateshead engine. On the right is the old loco. works No. 1 erecting shop.

Just about everything in this mid-1950's picture has now gone. York A2/3 4-6-2 No. 60512 "Steady Aim" heads the up Tees-Tyne Pullman over Naburn Swing bridge which carried the York-Selby line over the River Ouse. The locomotive was scrapped in 1966, while the bridge became a fixed structure – the cabin aloft disappearing – long before 1983 when the line itself was replaced by the East Coast main line diversion avoiding the new Selby coalfield.

Railway photography was illegal during the second world war but the author managed this rare shot of US Army Transportation Corps S160 2-8-0 No. 2107 on a freight near Naburn. The S160's followed the Allies into liberated Europe and may still be found in some countries.

Situated 10 miles south of York on the York and North Midland line to Normanton, Church Fenton station has changed little since Southern "Schools" 4-4-0 No. 30925 "Cheltenham" and Midland 2P 4-4-0 No. 40646 were photographed pausing there for water on 12th May 1962 with a Nottingham Victoria to Darlington railtour via Tadcaster and Ripon. Although the semaphore signals have been replaced and the water column has gone the station is much the same. Even "Cheltenham", now preserved by the National Railway Museum, has passed this way in recent years.

Until the 1960's Church Fenton was quite an operating centre, being the junction of three rail routes with a small marshalling yard and single road engine shed. On 9th September 1948, two steam cranes were engaged in track renewal work north of the station. On the left is the York-Normanton line, the Leeds line is in the centre and the Tadcaster/Wetherby line on the right. Of special interest is the motley collection of old rail vehicles in the yard.

(Stephen Chapman collection)

Above: Pairings of Birmingham/Sulzer Type 2 diesels (now class 26 or 27) were quite common on freight trains to and from York in the early 1960's. D5374 of Thornaby shed and an unidentified sister lead a southbound goods through Copmanthorpe.

Below: Copmanthorpe station was still very active when this picture was taken about 40 years ago. What appears to be a LNER J27 class 0-6-0 shunts the yard, but now the yard, station, signal box and semaphore signals have all gone, only the four fast running lines remaining. The village has grown into a major suburb of York but local pressure to have the station reopened has so far proved fruitless. *(Stephen Chapman collection)*

Copmanthorpe Moor level crossing no longer exists, having been closed ready for the opening of the Selby diversion in 1983 which saw numerous High Speed Trains routed through the village. Even so it ended up much modernised compared with this pre-war view of LNER B15 4-6-0 (ex-NER class S2) No. 840 on an up train of empty clerestory roofed coaches. On the left is the gate cabin where the author's father worked.

Below: In this rare pre-nationalisation picture a former Midland Railway Johnson class 3P 4-4-0, LMS No. 731 of Sheffield Millhouses shed, restarts a Sheffield Midland to York stopping train from Copmanthorpe. Today there is no trace of the station which can just be seen at the back of the train.

Above: LNER class 01 2-8-0 No. 3752 heads a southbound goods along the up Normanton line between Chaloner's Whin Junction and Copmanthorpe in the late 1940's. Bondhill Ash bridge carrying the main A64 Leed-Scarborough road in the background will soon be demolished to make room for overhead wires forming the East Coast main line electrification. A vast concrete flyover carrying the present A64 by-pass now stands about where the locomotive is. Note the neat ballast edge.

Below: Chaloner's Whin Junction, where the Selby line diverged from the Normanton line, ceased to exist in 1983 when the Selby diversion was opened and East Coast main line trains were routed via a new junction at Colton, south of Copmanthorpe. This view shows Chaloner's Whin some years before the 1951 resignalling as LMS Beyer-Garrat 2-6-6-2 No. 7992 approaches the signal box with a northbound iron ore train.

Above: In this magnificent pre-war view an unidentified LNER B15 4-6-0 speeds an express formed of old clerestory roofed coaches along the up Leeds line and away from Chaloner's Whin Junction.

Below: Well into BR days a rich variety of steam locomotives visited York. Here an ex-London and North Western Railway 0-8-0 has just passed Chaloner's Whin on its way into York with a train of bogie bolster wagons. The overbridge in the background replaced a level crossing, for which the keeper's cottage can still be seen.

Above: The Great Central Railway's chief mechanical engineer J. G. Robinson designed some fine 4-6-0's which reached York from time to time. In late LNER days class B8 No. 1355 leads a southbound goods between Dringhouses and Chaloner's Whin.

Below: A short distance north of the above shot and then in open country, LMS Black Five 4-6-0 No. 4781 gathers speed with a westbound express. Today houses line the railway on the left while the signal gantry is of course long gone.

Unusual pairings at Dringhouses. Above: In the 1950's Toton-based ex-LMS 4F 0-6-0 No. 44284 and a "Crab" 2-6-0 double head a mineral train bound for the Midlands past the old Dringhouses yard. Below: The Lowestoft-York express regularly brought East Anglian Britannia pacifics to York but in this early 1960's view two of the class, No. 70038 "Robin Hood" leading, head the return service past Dringhouses yard where modernisation is in progress.

In 1961 a new hump marshalling yard, the first in the country to deal with fully braked express freight trains, was opened at Dringhouses. It included a control tower from which the operator could route wagons into the appropriate sidings, using remotely controlled retarders to adjust their speed. The author worked on the yard's modernisation and took this photo as it neared completion.

A trio of freight trains await departure from Dringhouses yard in 1963 behind, from left, B1 4-6-0 No. 61198, B16/3 4-6-0 No. 61444 and WD 2-8-0 No. 90064. Dringhouses yard closed in 1987 when its work, dealing with air-braked Speedlink freight trains, was switched to Doncaster.

Passing beneath an impressive array of North Eastern slotted signals at South Points with an up mineral train in the late 1940's is former Midland Railway 4F 0-6-0, LMS No. 3885. The entrance to Dringhouses up yard is on the right and the exit from the few down sidings on the left. In the distance is South Points signal box and the entrance to Holgate reception sidings.

The LNER Thompson B1 4-6-0's were one of the more common locomotive classes at York, as witnessed by this late 1950's scene at South Points. No. 61321 plods along the Leeds line with a goods as she is overtaken by 61169 and another sister heading a southbound express on the Doncaster line. The author's gang has downed tools to let the cavalcade pass.

The celebrated class A4 pacifics were the mainstay of the most important expresses on the East Coast main line for over 25 years. The most famous of them all, world speed record holder No. 60022 "Mallard", passes Holgate reception sidings with the Newcastle to King's Cross "Northumbrian" in about 1950.

To see an A4 in such immaculate condition was becoming increasingly rare by the time No. 60028 "Walter K. Wigham" was photographed on Royal Train duty in 1961. No. 60028 was returning to London with the Queen and Duke of Edinburgh following the wedding of the Duke and Duchess of Kent at York Minster. The trees in the background – and no doubt the schoolgirls – have grown considerably since.

At Holgate Junction, just south of York station, was probably the most impressive array of NER slotted signals for miles around, as well as Holgate excursion platforms built to serve the city's racecourse. In this very early BR scene the very grimy V2 2-6-2 and its motley train contrast sharply with the famous up platform garden (still beautifully maintained despite the platform being closed 10 years before) and the freshly painted signals. On the left is the cabin housing the Holgate Junction ground frame which was electrically controlled from the Locomotive Yard box. The signal gantry and cabin disappeared with the 1951 resignalling but the platforms survived until 1964.

The Holgate signal gantry looks well overdue for its repaint in this pre-nationalisation view of LMS 4F 0-6-0 No. 4232 setting off with a return excursion from York station. The ramp behind leads to the down excursion platform.

The scene at Holgate looks somewhat bare following removal of the signal gantry and ramp in 1951. Not long afterwards a Sheffield express leaves York behind former Great Central "Large Director" (LNER class D11/1) 4-4-0 No. 62663 "Prince Albert" of Sheffield Darnall shed.

Several years after the above picture, in 1958, un-named Patriot 4-6-0 No. 45517 of Bank Hall (Liverpool) shed is in charge of a Newcastle-Liverpool express formed of new BR Mk1 coaches. This train was a survivor of the old Lancashire and Yorkshire Railway, running via Wakefield and the L & Y main line.

Above: 1962 and the famous Deltics make their debut. No. D9004 hauls the newly introduced Edinburgh-King's Cross "Talisman" express beneath "Dickie Bridge" – a footbridge still popular with railway enthusiasts and photographers.

Below: Pulling the crowds at Holgate Junction on 29th April 1978 are preserved Black Fives Nos. 45407 and 44932 with a return special to Carnforth. The spectators are stood on the once extensive Holgate cattle docks which today lay derelict and trackless.

Some years before the production Deltics went into service, the prototype "Deltic" ran trials through York as pictured here.

With York South motive power depot and the lines to York Yards in the background, Brush Type 2 diesels (now class 31) Nos D5680 and D5685 leave York in the late 1950's with an express bound for the Western Region. On the left is the roofless ex-Midland Railway roundhouse while the roof of the remaining small NER roundhouse protrudes above the locomotives.

The author's gang was among the men working on this relaying project at York South in the late 1940's. The old Locomotive Yard signal box is on the left and the former Queen Street works on the right.

This 1940's scene shows just how busy York used to be and how the station's south approaches were enclosed by buildings and structures. Today with gantries, signal box and loco sheds long since swept away the area is surrounded instead by wide open spaces. The south sheds can be seen on the left behind the signal box and Queen Street shed on the right as a grimy V2 2-6-2 leaves the station with a southbound express.

Above: LMS Black Five 4-6-0 No. 5315 is overshadowed by the signal gantries of York South as it marshalls a pair of coaches which it will attach to its Manchester express. Behind is the huge Locomotive Yard signal box which existed from 1909 to 1951 and had 295 levers. The second gantry was also a staff footbridge leading to the signal box and loco depot.

Below: A similar operation to that above but in the early 1960's by which time the scene has changed quite dramatically. BR Standard "Britannia 4-6-2 No. 70035 "Rudyard Kipling" waits with a rather venerable dining car before taking over a Newcastle-Colchester express. The by then disused small roundhouse is visible but the signal box and gantries disappeared with the 1951 resignalling.

Above: Looking south through a forest of slotted signals from platform eight. Note the huge hoarding on the opposite platform. *(Stephen Chapman collection)*

Below: In very early BR days A2 4-6-2 No. 60532 "Blue Peter" drifts past Queen Street shed en route to the North shed after bringing in an up express. On Queen Street shed are a V2 2-6-2 and D49/2 4-4-0 No. E2770 "The Puckeridge" (The "E" was used on Eastern and North Eastern Region locomotives for a short time after nationalisation before the "6" was added to the old LNER number.) Formerly the works boiler shop, Queen Street shed was taken over by the Lancashire and Yorkshire Railway but closed by the LMS in the 1930's when that company took up residence at the South sheds. It was then used for stabling locomotives, latterly on standby for diesel failures, until the mid-1960's. A 1950's proposal for the shed to become a diesel depot was not permanently adopted and it was used for stabling officers' saloons until 1968 when the roof fell in, writing off one saloon. The shed was demolished shortly after.

The 1841 Great North of England locomotive shed forming part of the York South MPD miraculously survived until 1963 albeit much rebuilt. The Great Northern Railway used the shed after the NER opened its new depot at York North in 1877 and then the LMS moved in from Queen Street shed in the 1930's. In LMS days a Stanier 8F 2-8-0 and Beyer-Garratt 2-6-6-2 No. 7968 are seen stabled there between duties.

From closure as a running shed until demolition in 1963 the shed was used for storing locomotives awaiting scrapping or major repairs. Ex-NER class S3 (LNER B16/1) 4-6-0 No. 61452 was out of use there with a J27 0-6-0 in 1961.

Diesels at York South shed were rare indeed. Brand new Sulzer Type 2 (later class 24) No. D5096 stands outside the old GNE shed in 1958.

For a short time until 1961 the closed south shed was used for stabling York station and yard pilots. J72 0-6-0T No. 68677 and ex-LMS 3F 0-6-0T No. 47334 stand in the by then roofless ex-Midland roundhouse. *(N. E. Stead)*

Behind the Queen Street shed in the former works complex was a 60ft turntable which remained in use well into the 1960's. It is pictured (above) being used between the wars by ex-North Eastern Q class 4-4-0 No. 1905, and (below) by well-kept class C7 (NER class Z) 4-4-2 No. 2972 in the late 1940's. Behind the Atlantic are the works No. 1 and 2 erecting shops. No. 2 shop was converted into the Railway Institute gymnasium in 1926, a role it still fulfills today.

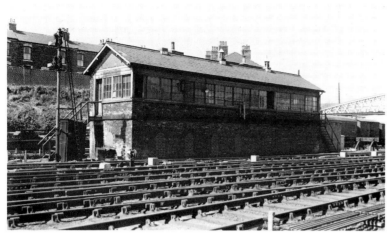

The freight avoiding lines through York Yards were not included in the 1951 resignalling and this old mechanical box at York Yard South survived until 1962 when this picture was taken. *(BR Eastern Region)*. It was replaced by an electric box on the opposite side of the line (below) being passed by a diesel shunter hauling a train consisting mainly of brake vans. The footbridge linked the carriage and wagon works and was subsequently removed. York Yard is behind.

When opened in 1951 the present York signal box controlled the biggest route relay interlocking system in the world, covering over 33 miles of track. In May 1989 it will give way to a new electronic system controlling over 200 miles.

York wagon works closed in the mid 1960's though part still survives as a regional wagon and crane repair depot. The works is seen in 1960 when still busy with a wide variety of wagons. *(BR Eastern Region)*

A 1964 view of the body shop in York carriage works. The works was established in 1884 and remains busy today, building new electric commuter trains. Later in 1988 it was due to be sold into private ownership under the privatisation of its owners, British Rail Engineering Ltd. *(BR Eastern Region)*

Two panoramic views taken in 1964 of York carriage works which still stretches almost the full length of York Yards. Above: at the north end looking south with a selection of contemporary containers in for repair. Below: Coaches of all kinds and ages fill the huge yard next to Poppleton Road which is today much reduced and partly covered by the works car park. Note the immaculate restaurant car on the left and the traverser in the foreground. *(Both BR Eastern Region)*

A part of the railway scene once familiar but no longer extant was the express horse box, like this one seen under repair at the road motor shops on 31st January, 1961. Converted from the Queen Street works machine shop earlier this century the RME shop still exists although not now under railway ownership. In 1972 it was transferred to National Carriers along with BR's freight sundries and road delivery operations and is today used for the BRS contract vehicle maintenance service. (*BR Eastern Region*)

Also transferred to the road-orientated National Carriers in 1972 was the Leeman Road goods depot, pictured on 31st January, 1961. Vast quantities of general merchandise which mostly goes by road nowadays were handled but the traffic was unprofitable for the railway which was glad to be rid of it. When the depot was vested in NCL BR concentrated its freight activity at Foss Islands. Rail traffic quickly disappeared at Leeman Road and NCL eventually pulled out too. The building was taken over by the National Railway Museum which now uses it for the storage and restoration of exhibits. (*BR Eastern Region*)

The original 1841 station was still being used for stabling coaching stock when this picture was taken on 20th September, 1960. On the left, below the city wall, is the loading bay for car carrier services, later known as Motorail, while to the right is an elderly goods warehouse known locally as the sack warehouse. Note the wagon turntable giving side access to the building. Dominating the skyline is the 1906 NER headquarters building, by this time the headquarters of BR's NE Region. In front of it, along the platform ends is the 1853 hotel which later became part of the office complex along with the old station buildings. In 1966 all track was lifted, part of the station roof demolished and the Motorail terminal moved to the "new" station's platform 1 to make way for a new technical office block called Hudson House. (*BR Eastern Region*)

A late 1950's close-up of the old twin wagon turntables leading into the sack warehouse. The track inside the warehouse has already been removed.

One of the earliest photos taken by the author shows Great Northern Stirling 4-2-2 No. 1 and a train of four or six-wheel coaches exhibited at the old station in 1925. The event was to mark the centenary of the Stockton and Darlington Railway.

In the early 1950's A4 4-6-2 No. 60003 "Andrew K. McCosh" collects the stock of its excursion from the old station. The picture is not dated but the union flag on the headquarters building suggests it is a day of national celebration.

Above: Contrast at York – grimy J72 0-6-0T station pilot No. 68686 stands on the through line between platforms 14 and 15 next to Brush Type 2 diesel No. D5547.

Below: In the opposite condition to the above J72 is No. 68736 which was lovingly restored to North Eastern green livery and always kept immaculate. It worked at York on front line passenger pilot duties until 1961 before being transferred to Newcastle where it worked alongside similarly restored 68723 until the end of 1963.

The splendid arched roof which tops York station is today beautifully restored and a tourist attraction in its own right, but when this picture was taken in the mid 1960's it was still blackened by the soot and grime of the steam age. Like any big station in those days, however, it had a rich and unique atmosphere which was abundantly evident as preserved LNER A3 pacific No. 4472 "Flying Scotsman" prepared to hand over a northbound railtour to Southern Region Merchant Navy class No. 35026 "Lamport and Holt Lines."

REGULAR EXCURSIONS

FROM
YORK, HARROGATE, SCARBOROUGH, SELBY and DISTRICT

17th JUNE TO 8th SEPTEMBER 1963

The frontage of York station in 1965. Note the old traffic bollards, contemporary posters, and the sign pointing to the car sleeper loading dock at the old station. The Royal Station Hotel, sold into private ownership in 1983, is in the background. (*BR Eastern Region*)

Above: Edinburgh Haymarket based class D49/1 4-4-0 No. 62705 "Lanarkshire" waits to leave platform 12 with a stopping train to either Harrogate or Darlington in very early BR days. Of interest on the platform is the water cart used for topping up restaurant car supplies.

Below: Original Great Eastern Railway Holden class B12 4-6-0 No. 1561 awaits the right away from platform 7 in the immediate post war years with what is almost certainly the 10.10 am express to Hull via Market Weighton. This train was at the time formed of air braked stock and was diagrammed for a Doncaster locomotive which necessitated the use of a B12 fitted with air-brake pumps.

In more recent years York station has been the set for railway scenes in a number of films, including Chariots of Fire, and Agatha, a story about Agatha Christie starring Dustin Hoffman and Vanessa Redgrave. Above: during the filming of Agatha in November 1977 platforms 4-7 were disguised as Harrogate station and Flying Scotsman as sister engines Nos. 4474 "Victor Wild" (on one side) and 4480 "Enterprise" (on the other). Preserved J72 0-6-0T No. 69023 "JoEm" was also on the set, recalling the days when the class were regular York pilots.

Below: For filming a new Ovaltine commercial in 1981 preserved Midland Railway compound 4-4-0 No. 1000 was used with authentic rolling stock. The roof end screens were renewed with glass and alloy in 1972-3, and although as faithfully reproduced as possible with modern materials there is still quite a difference when compared with the wooden originals shown on the previous page. (*Stephen Chapman*)

English Electric Type 4 diesels (class 40) made their debut on the East Coast main line in 1958 and on Liverpool-Newcastle expresses in 1960. No. D259 is shown heading a northbound express out of platform 14 in 1960. The 1951 signal box can be seen towering above the first four coaches.

Pictured heading out of platform 16 in the early 1960's is "The South Yorkshireman" railtour from Halifax to Darlington. The train is hauled by No. 52515, one of the delightful Aspinall Lancashire and Yorkshire 0-6-0's based at Sowerby Bridge, and LMS 4F 0-6-0 No. 44408.

Above: In the early days of British Railways, class A3 4-6-2 No. 60045 "Lemberg" hauls a northbound express over Waterworks crossing which linked York Yards and the west side platforms with the Scarborough line. On the left is Leeman Road signal box which had 91 levers, and to the right a temporary Waterworks box replacing the original which was demolished in 1938 to make room for track alterations.

Below: The Elizabethan was the top East Coast express of the 1950's, covering the 393 mile Kings Cross-Edinburgh run without a single stop – except on this occasion when A4 No. 60030 "Golden Fleece" had to pause north of York station for water.

Waterworks crossing was renewed in October 1961, a major project – as seen in these pictures – in which a good deal of muscle power was used. If the job was being done today the site would be levelled by sophisticated laser-guided machines. In the background of the lower picture is the old pumphouse which extracted the railway's water supply from the River Ouse below. (*Both Stephen Chapman collection*)

In 1957/58 two of the four North locomotive roundhouses were replaced by a new straight shed equipped with the best facilities ranging from overhead cranes and illuminated inspection pits to a wheel drop for removing locomotive wheels. Not surprisingly it became the diesel depot and continued in business until 1982. It was later sold to the National Railway Museum which now uses it for maintaining and repairing exhibits. Above: construction work in progress. Below: (*BR Eastern Region*) Inside the shed on 1st December, 1966 with diesel shunters, a class 40 diesel, K1 2-6-0 and recently withdrawn A4 No. 60019 "Bittern" awaiting private preservation.

Above: After the 1957 North shed modernisation the surviving twin roundhouse remained a busy running shed for 10 more years. Among the many steam locomotives gathered round its 60 and 70ft turntables in 1964 were A1 4-6-2 No 60155 "Borderer", K1 2-6-0 No. 62065 and WD 2-8-0 No. 90517.

Below: Just two and a half years later, in December 1966, the steam age is coming to a close so far as York shed is concerned. It holds just a K1 2-6-0, a B1 4-6-0, a pair of diesel shunters, a snowplough and, at the back, York's last V2 2-6-2 No. 60831. Seven months later the shed was closed to steam but continued to be used for stabling diesels and departmental rolling stock until 1973 when it closed altogether for conversion to the National Railway Museum's main exhibiton hall. Ironically, steam locomotives once again cluster round its twin turntables. (*BR Eastern Region*)

Above: York North shed officially closed to steam on 25th June, 1967 though facilities remained for servicing visiting steam locomotives until the complete end of steam on BR in 1968. Upon closure York's surviving handful of working steam locomotives, such as Standard class 3 2-6-0 No. 77012, seen on the last day, were transferred to other depots, mainly in the Bradford area. (*Stephen Chapman*)

Steam was still king and the closure of York North depot unimaginable in late LNER days when diminutive class Y8 0-4-0T No. 8091, built by the NER in 1890, was shed pilot.

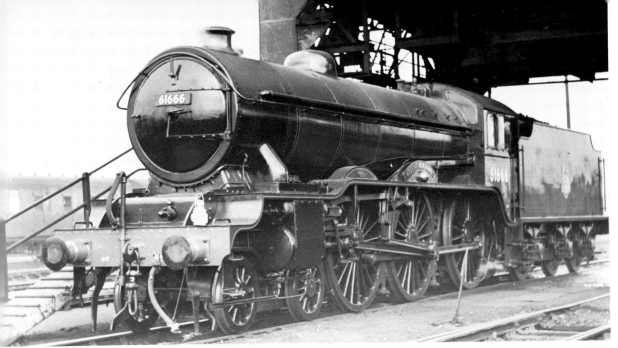

Until the BR Britannia pacifics came on the scene ex-LNER class B17 4-6-0's, like Cambridge-based No. 61666 "Nottingham Forest", seen under York coaling plant in the early 1950's, regularly worked services from the Eastern counties.

Also regular visitors to York, with iron ore trains from Wellingborough to Teesside, were the unusual Crosti-boilered class 9F 2-10-0's, such as No. 92027 pictured in the North shed yard. These locomotives had a flue beneath the boiler which used hot exhaust gases to pre-heat the feedwater, thereby improving thermal efficiency. As a result the chimney was at the back end of the boiler, the one visible in the usual place being purely cosmetic.

Coaled up and ready to head for King's Cross with that most famous of summer holiday trains, The Scarborough Flyer, is class A2 4-6-2 No. 60526 "Sugar Palm". The A2 is seen at the north end of the yard.

As part of a package of improvements at the York North depot a 70ft electric turntable was installed at the north end of the yard in 1932. It is seen being used by Willesden-based Britannia 4-6-2 No. 70020 "Mercury" which had arrived with an enthusiast's special.

York's mechanical coaling plant, overshadowing grimy pacifics Nos. 60138 "Boswell" and 60040 "Cameronian", was also built in 1932. Made of reinforced concrete, it was a notable landmark until being demolished, with considerable difficulty, in 1970. A3 No. 60040 had just arrived from London with The Norseman, a boat train to Newcastle which connected with sailings for Scandinavia.

Stabled in Clifton down sidings in the early 1950's was elderly 6-wheeled officers' saloon No. E900269E. The tin shed in the right background, on the other side of the main line, is the Clifton carriage washer which dated from the 1920's. Despite its decrepit appearance it survived rather longer than its electronic successor which was commissioned in 1984 and closed, along with the brand new depot, in 1987!

For 10 years The Elizabethan was the crack East Coast main line express, covering the 393-mile King's Cross-Edinburgh journey non-stop in 6½ hours. Above, in the 1950's, it passes York North motive power depot behind A4 No. 60010 "Dominion of Canada" and (below) in 1962, behind new Deltic No. D9002. (*Both C. Ord*)

Class A3 4-6-2 No. 60091 "Captain Cuttle" heads a down express past Clifton shortly after nationalisation. The attractive trackside borders were a feature of the York railway scene then which would be most welcome today.

Ruston 88hp diesel shunter No. 84 belonged to the Chief Civil Engineer's department and was kept at Leeman Road permanent way yard in the 1960's for shunting.

Above: J27 0-6-0's built from 1906 onwards were not seen at York in great numbers but were nevertheless prominent on local goods workings. Here, No. 65849 of Malton shed, shunts at Skelton sidings next to the sugar factory.

Below: Skelton New Yard, built with Government money in the 1940's to help meet the war effort, was the northern extremity of the York railway complex until being abandoned in the 1970's. It incorporated locomotive servicing facilities, including a 70ft turntable seen being used in 1948 by class A2/1 4-6-2 No. 60509 "Waverley".

The first of the great streamlined expresses of the 1930's, The Silver Jubilee, was introduced in 1935 along with Sir Nigel Gresley's famous A4 pacifics. One of the first Silver Jubilee runs hauled by pioneer A4 No. 2509 "Silver Link" was photographed north of York by the author.

The magnificent spectacle of double-headed North Eastern Railway Atlantics on the famous racetrack north of York. The train engine is a class Z (LNER C7) dating from around 1911, but the leading engine is an earlier type, probably NER class V.

A few miles north of York was Beningbrough station, closed in September, 1958. In disgrace in the adjacent goods yard, which survived another seven years, is A4 4-6-2 No. 60006 "Sir Ralph Wedgewood" after failing with the Tees-Tyne Pullman.

Unusually north of York, an ex-Great Central 0-8-0 of LNER class Q4, heads a southbound coal train through Tollerton in early BR days. The station, closed on 1st November, 1965, can just be seen at the back of the train.

Above: The glory of the streamline era on the North main line. A4 No. 2512 "Silver Fox" speeds the northbound Flying Scotsman towards Tollerton in the mid-1930's.

Below: Parts of the main line north of York had only three tracks until widening took place in the 1950's. Here, A4 No. 60011 "Empire of India" races north over a three-track section with the Elizabethan.

Above: Pilmoor station 16 miles north of York was a pure railway junction serving only passengers changing between the branches from Knaresborough and Ryedale and the main line. In early BR days and with resignalling under way, class K3/2 2-6-0 No. 61984 passes through with a northbound goods. The Knaresborough branch platform is on the right. Pilmoor station closed to passengers on 5th May, 1958 and to goods on 14th September, 1959.

Below: Passing p.way work at Pilmoor with a northbound express are LNER D20/1 4-4-0 (NER class R1) No. 2390 and a V2 2-6-2.

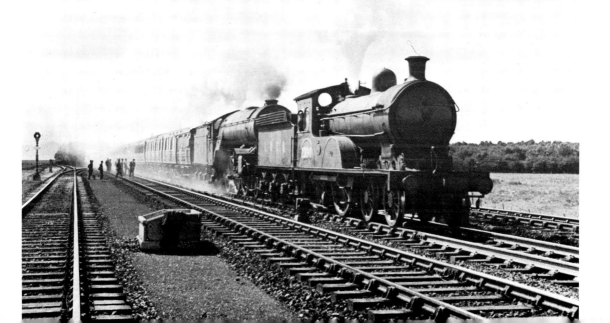

Above: Just over a mile from York station is Burton Lane Junction, where the branch to Foss Islands freight terminal leaves the Scarborough line. The junction and branch may well have gone by 1989 and the signal box, one of the last mechanical boxes in the York area, will certainly disappear under the 1988/89 resignalling. Preserved LMS Black Five 4-6-0 No. 5305 storms past Burton Lane box with the Scarborough Spa Express BR steam service on 15th August, 1982. (*Stephen Chapman*)

Below: Apart from the daily DMU service to Rowntree's Halt for workers at the confectionary factory, passenger trains on the Foss Islands branch have been few and far between. On 12th April, 1977 London and North Western 2-4-0 No. 790 "Hardwicke", of the National Railway Museum, heads a Yorkshire Television special bound for the Derwent Valley Railway away from Burton Lane Junction. In the left background (and close-up right) is a NER slotted signal which, at the time of going to press, is probably the last of its kind.

Rowntree's Halt was opened in 1927 for workers and visitors travelling to the confectionary factory. After 61 years it now looks certain to close in 1988 after the local Transport Users' Consultative Committee raised no objection to a proposal by BR for withdrawal of its daily train to and from Selby. In 1982 a 3-car DMU awaits departure with the 16.40 to Selby. (*Stephen Chapman*)

The Rowntree-Mackintosh factory produced very heavy freight traffic until April 1987 when the company abruptly switched all its distribution arrangements to juggernaut lorries – a sad occasion for the city and its railway which hastened the decline of the Foss Islands branch. When this picture was taken of class 20 diesel 20035 reversing a long rake of air braked vans into the factory in April 1983, the works was served by at least two trips a day from Dringhouses yard. (*Stephen Chapman*)

Foss Islands freight depot was still busy handling respectable quantities of solid fuel, sand and soda ash (for the nearby glassworks), agricultural products and general freight when this picture was taken in 1979. When the glassworks closed the line, opened in 1879 to convey cattle to the adjacent market, lost most of its traffic and the depot closed in 1986. In 1988 the only traffic left was an infrequent domestic oil train to what is left of the Derwent Valley Railway (left), while the yard on the right is now a DIY superstore.

The Derwent Valley Light Railway opened in 1913 and ran 16 miles to Cliff Common where it connected with the Selby-Market Weighton line. Escaping nationalisation, it remained privately-owned to the end, serving the rural communities along the way for nearly 70 years – and at a profit. The DVLR's York terminus and headquarters was Layerthorpe station, next to Foss Islands BR yard. It was photographed in 1979, a time when a steam passenger service was being run for tourists. (*Malcolm Roughley*)

In 1977, 52 years after the end of regular passenger services, the DVR started running a steam service in a bid to attract the tourist trade. Although the service was moderately successful, the line's shortage of scenic attributes did little for its future development and it lasted only three seasons. Preserved J72 0-6-0T No. 69023 "JoEm" was bought by the DVR to operate the service, bringing the class back to York after an absence of 16 years. This was the rustic scene after the service had been withdrawn and "JoEm" was stored for a time in the DVR's "lean-to" shed. (*Malcolm Roughley*)

A mid-1950's railtour threads its way through the Tang Hall district along the weed-covered DVR behind Darlington-based J21 0-6-0 No. 65064.

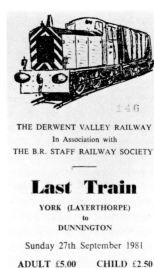

Murton Lane level crossing provides a truly rural setting in 1979 as "JoEm" heads an afternoon service to Dunnington. The driver is Geoff Bird, a former York shedmaster. The crossing has now gone but a few hundred yards of track towards Murton village has been incorporated into the Yorkshire Museum of Farming. (*Stephen Chapman*)

The official last train on the DVR ran on 27th September, 1981. Organised by the British Rail Staff Railway Society, it consisted of four BR Mk1 coaches hauled by the railway's ex-BR Drewry 0-6-0 diesel "Lord Wenlock" (left.) The train is being marshalled at Dunnington, the line's final terminus, by 1933 Fowler 0-4-0 diesel "Winston Churchill" which belonged to Yorkshire Grain Dryers Ltd., a major DVR customer. Lord Wenlock's adornments were provided by the author. (*Stephen Chapman*)

Dunnington, the source of heavy barley traffic to Scottish distillieries, was the railway's terminus from 1973 until final closure. "JoEm" stands at the buffers on 14th May, 1977 after arriving with the 14.30 from Layerthorpe. (*Stephen Chapman*)

From 1968 until the cutback to Dunnington on 19th January, 1973, the DVR's terminus was at Elvington where this old Manchester, Sheffield and Lincolnshire 6-wheeled coach was photographed in 1964. Towards the end Elvington handled mostly fertilizer traffic and was used for storing 100 ton tank wagons. (*Stephen Chapman*)

A little over half way from Layerthorpe to Cliff Common, Wheldrake, pictured here in 1964, was one of the more important stations on the DVR. It became the terminus on 22nd February, 1965 with closure of the line beyond and closed on 19th June, 1968 with the cutback to Elvington. (*Stephen Chapman*)

Next station down the line and 11½ miles from York was Thorganby, pictured in 1951. The ex-South Eastern and Chatham Railway 6-wheel brake van is now preserved on the Bluebell Railway. (*R. B. Parr*)

Above: The old North Eastern Railway survivor with a late 1940's Whitby to York train on the Scarborough line near Strensall is class A6 4-6-2T No. 9799. These locomotives were rebuilt in 1915 from earlier 4-6-0T's.

Below: Until replaced by 4-6-0's in the late 1940's the ex-NER class Z Atlantics (LNER class C7) were the mainstay of Leeds-Scarborough expresses. An early morning train from Scarborough rounds the curve at Flaxton on newly relaid track behind No. 2986 after just having passed a goods going the other way.

Above: P.way work halts as class V2 2-6-2 No. 60847 "St. Peter's School York, AD627" heads an express for Scarborough in late LNER days. Note the horseboxes behind the engine which were a regular feature of Scarborough line trains. Were they carrying racehorses for stables around Malton or donkeys for the beach?

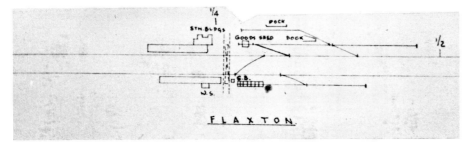

Below: Near Flaxton and snow wasn't allowed to stop work in pick and shovel days.

Above: One of several attractive stations on the Scarborough line was Hutton's Ambo which closed, as did many smaller stations, in September 1930. It remained beautifully maintained in the mid-1950's when B1 4-6-0 No. 61016 "Inyala" was caught racing through with a holiday express.

Below: The pick-up goods calling at wayside stations and often employing veteran locomotives is now virtually extinct. LNER class J25 0-6-0 No. 5679 leaves Hutton's Ambo with a York-Malton working shortly after the second world war.

Malton was once an important railway centre on the Scarborough line and its small but busy motive power depot supplied locomotives not only for the main line but for branches to Whitby, Ryedale and Driffield. Above: Vintage locomotives on view in the early days of BR are, from left: J21 0-6-0 No. 5121, a class A6 or A7 4-6-2T, J24 0-6-0 No. 65642 and G5 0-4-4T No. 7349. The shed closed in 1963 and today little more than the station itself remains.

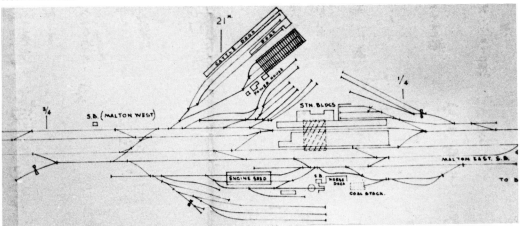

Below: With the station in the background, G5 0-4-4T No. 7294 stands in Malton's small yard.